LOOK WHAT WE'VE BROUGHT YOU FROM

INDIA

CRAFTS, GAMES, RECIPES, STORIES,
AND OTHER CULTURAL ACTIVITIES FROM
INDIAN AMERICANS

PHYLLIS
SHALANT

JULIAN MESSNER
PARSIPPANY, NEW JERSEY

Photo Credits

All photographs by Silver Burdett Ginn (SBG) unless otherwise noted.

Anthony Blake Photo Library/Merehurst: 6-7. Aspect Picture Library, Ltd./Katia Natola: 11. Art Resource, NY/SEF: 36. The Bridgeman Art Library/National Museum of India, New Delhi: 38. © The British Library: 37. Corbis Media: 15. Dinodia Picture Agency/B.D. Garekar: 10 *t.*; P.R. Gansham: 46; Milind Ketkar: 21; Firoze Mistry: 20; G.C. Patel: 45; Suraj N. Sharma: cover *inset*; Ravi Shekhar: 34. From the collection of Dr. Irving Finkel: 24. Arvind Garg: 30. The John Hillelson Agency/Roland & Sabrina Michaud: 16, 25. Wolfgang Kaehler: 14. Paul W. Liebhardt: 3. Robert Harding Picture Library: 4. Uniphoto Picture Agency/Ajay Salvi: 10 *b*. By courtesy of the Board of Trustees of the Victoria & Albert Museum: 41. Viesti Associates, Inc./Dinodia: 12; Luca Tettoni: 32. © 1997 Woodfin Camp & Associates/Lindsay Hebberd: 17.

Illustrations: Kara Fellows.
Map, flag: Ortelius Design.

Library of Congress Cataloging-in-Publication Data
Shalant, Phyllis.
    Look what we've brought you from India: crafts, games, recipes, stories, and other cultural activities from Indian Americans/by Phyllis Shalant.
    p. cm.
    Summary: Introduces the culture of India, describing important holidays, customs, special arts, folktales, games, and foods.
    ISBN 0-382-39463-1 (lsb).—ISBN 0-382-39465-8 (pbk.)
    1. India—Civilization—Juvenile literature. 2. India—Social life and customs—Juvenile literature. 3. East Indian Americans—Social life and customs—Juvenile literature. [1. India—Social life and customs.] I. Title.
    DS421.S494 1998   97-414
    954—dc21

Copyright © 1998 by Phyllis Shalant

Cover and book design by Michelle Farinella

Published by Julian Messner
A Division of Simon & Schuster
299 Jefferson Road, Parsippany, NJ 07054

First Edition
Printed in the United States of America
10 9 8 7 6 5 4 3 2 1

A c k n o w l e d g m e n t s

So many people gave generously of their time and knowledge to support the writing of this book. The Indian-American Cultural Society of Westchester, New York, first helped me make contact with Dr. Kiritida Shah from Gujarat, who opened her home to me. Dr. Shah taught me how to cook a *chapati*, how to play Five Shells, and how a *rangoli* is made, among other things. My neighbor, Mary Alencherril, from Kerala, read parts of the manuscript, made suggestions, and provided reference books and art sources. At our local Indian-Pakistani grocery, I met Amarjeet Ahuja from New Delhi, who introduced me to ghee, cardamom, and *burfee*, a popular Indian candy. Sumita Bhattacharya, from Bihar, remembered the poem by Rabindranath Tagore, which is familiar to children all over India. Nivedita Garabadu, from Orissa, read the manuscript for accuracy and offered recipes. The Indian Consulate in New York City allowed me access to their library. Finally, staff members of the Smithsonian Museum of Natural History in Washington, D.C., and of the Brooklyn Museum, New York, helped me track down the multimedia kit *Aditi: The Living Arts of India*, which helped me begin my journey. Thanks to one and all!

Where the mind is without fear and the head is held high;

Where knowledge is free;

Where the world has not been broken up into fragments

by narrow domestic walls;

Where words come out from the depth of truth;

Where tireless striving stretches its arms towards perfection;

Where the clear stream of reason has not lost its way into the

dreary desert sand of dead habit;

Where the mind is led forward by thee into ever-widening

thought and action—

Into that heaven of freedom, my Father, let my country awake.

Gitanjali, XXXV
Rabindranath Tagore,
winner of the Nobel Prize for Literature,
1913

Contents

INTRODUCTION

6
India: Spice of Life • 7

HOLIDAY FUN!

10
Diwali, Festival of Lights • 11
Make a Lantern for Diwali • 12
Republic Day, January 26 • 14
Mahatma Gandhi, Peaceful Protester • 15
Holi, the Spring Festival • 16
Raksha Bandhan: Ties of Protection • 18

GAMES

Kabaddi • 20
Ghora Baddi • 22
Pachisi • 24
Pawa Duree • 26
Five Shells • 28

SPECIAL ARTS

Mehndi: Hand Painting • 30
Rangoli: Floor Painting • 32
Make a Floor Painting • 33
Tie-Dyeing • 34

INDIAN STORIES

Tales From the *Ramayana* • 36
A Tale From the *Mahabharata* • 40

LET'S EAT

Chapati • 42
Aloo Mattar • 44
Coconut Burfee • 46
Bibliography • 48
Index • 48

Namaste! This Hindi greeting is one of the most popular ways of saying hello in India, but it is certainly not the only way. Although Hindi and English are the two official languages of this huge country, the people of India speak 15 different major languages, more than 300 minor languages, and approximately 3,000 dialects! And it is the same with religion. Although 80 percent of India's people are Hindu, the country is also home to Muslims, Christians, Sikhs, Buddhists, Jains, Jews, and Zoroastrians. So it is no wonder there are so many different voices to be heard. India has the second largest population on Earth—over 835 million people. That means that every sixth person in the world is Indian.

What brings so many individuals together to make a single nation? One answer is a way of thinking based on ancient songs, fables, traditions, and customs. Much of this rich culture has been transported to the United States by Indian immigrants who have incorporated it into their special Indian American style of living.

Of the more than 815,000 Indian Americans today, about 245,000 are children. You may have Indian American friends in your community, or even classmates with whom you can play some of the games in this book, such as *Ghora Baddi.* You might want to celebrate *Raksha Bandhan,* the special Indian holiday for sisters and brothers. Or perhaps you'll welcome new Indian Americans to your school with *Namaste!*

Located in southern Asia, the Republic of India is only one-third the size of the United States. But it has more than ten times as many people per square mile (689, India; 68, U.S.). Its three largest cities are Calcutta on the east coast (population: 9,165,650); Bombay on the west coast (population: 8,227,332); and in the north, the capital city of New Delhi (population: 5,350,928). Despite the large cities, most Indians still live in the country's 600,000 rural villages.

In addition to more people, India also has more kinds of weather than most places. Although the majority of the country has three seasons—hot, wet, and cool—six seasons can actually be found: winter, spring, summer, summer monsoon, autumn, and winter monsoon. Although monsoon winds bring much-needed daily rains to the country, they often cause great floods.

India: Spice of Life

Water is very important to India in another way as well. The Ganges River, which flows down from the Himalayas in the northern plains, is considered the sacred river of India. Many religious celebrations, such as the world's largest festival, the Kumbha Mela, revolve around the Ganges. Every two out of three Indians live along the flat plains of the Ganges, where the land is good for farming.

If variety is the spice of life, India is the spiciest country in the world. Each of the nation's 25 states has its own language, culture, customs, style of dress, and way of cooking, so learning what Indian culture is about is quite a challenge! The many differences are due in part to the land's long history. India claims one of the earliest great civilizations known to humankind, the Indus Valley civilization, which was established over 5,000 years ago. There the people lived in great cities that had elaborate houses, broad roads, and even drainage systems. They farmed, produced textiles, and traded with their western neighbors.

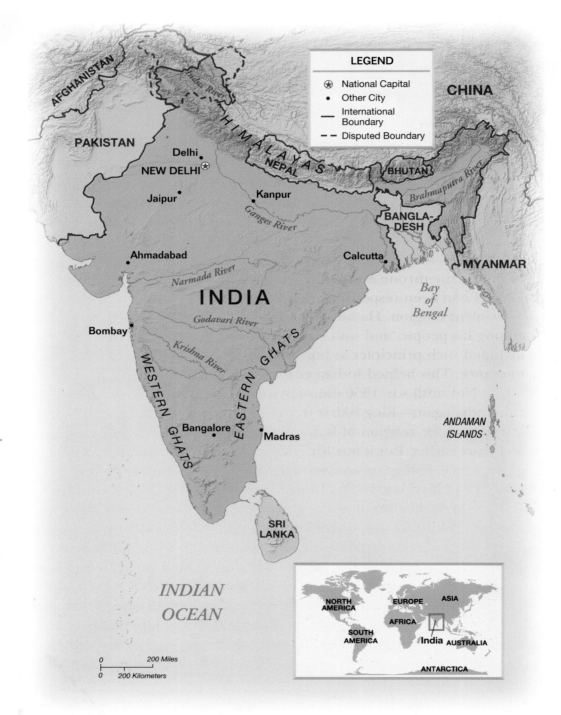

LEGEND

⊛ National Capital
• Other City
— International Boundary
- - Disputed Boundary

However, beginning in approximately 1750 B.C., the rich and prosperous cities of the Indus Valley were invaded by a warlike people from northeastern Europe known as the Aryans, who fought on horseback and in chariots. The Aryans spread their religion, Hinduism, along with their beliefs and customs, throughout the continent.

Perhaps the next greatest influence on the culture of India came from King Asoka, who ascended the throne around 274 B.C. Horrified by bloody wars he himself had been responsible for, Asoka converted to Buddhism, a nonviolent religion. He helped to foster the growth of Buddhism among his people, and with it a strict code of ethical conduct that included such principles as honesty, charity, justice, and religious tolerance. This helped Indian culture to flourish.

Not until A.D. 1556 did such a brilliant and thoughtful king rule India again—King Akbar of the Mogul Empire. The Moguls introduced the religion of Islam to India when they arrived some 300 years earlier. But it was King Akbar who brought many religious, social, and governmental reforms to India and promoted the idea of a unified nation. Yet India would still be ruled by another foreign culture before it would gain independence.

In the 1600s the British, seeking such riches as silk and spices, gained control of India. They set up factories and introduced new systems of government and education, as well as another religion, Christianity. Finally, in 1885, a group of Indians formed the Indian National Congress, later led by Mohandas K. Gandhi, which was dedicated to the creation of a unified and independent nation. The India that was on its way to self-rule was a patchwork of thousands of years of ideas, beliefs, cultures, and customs, making it the diverse and fascinating nation we know today.

Hinduism is a complex, rich religion with many gods and goddesses. The major events in Hinduism are usually remembered by a holiday. Most Indians celebrate these holidays with feasts, fairs, music, or dance, or all of these! Some of these combine *utsavas*, religious festivals that celebrate divine happenings, and *melas*, fairs that mix religion, shopping, and entertainment. At melas, people view puppet shows, circuses, magicians, and livestock races, as well as dramas, songs, and dances derived from Hinduism, India's main religion. Temporary markets or bazaars are set up. These feature rural crafts, fabrics, and other goods that are not always available in villages. Shelters are set up for visitors who may come from long distances. With so many religions in one country, utsavas and melas are frequent occurrences in Indian life.

Folk dances are a part of many Indian festivals.

Diwali is a Hindu festival that marks the end of the monsoon and the harvesting of rainy season crops. Like all Hindu festivals, the timing of the celebration is determined by the lunar calendar, so Diwali may fall in October or November on the night of the new moon.

Diwali, Festival of Lights

At Diwali, homes, temples, and public buildings are lit with thousands of oil lamps and electric lights to welcome Lakshmi, the Hindu goddess of wealth and prosperity. In preparation for the holiday, families clean and decorate their homes, buy new clothes, and prepare great feasts. Sweets and symbols of wealth are set around statues of Lakshmi to ask the goddess's blessing. In the evening, fireworks light up the sky.

You can't celebrate Diwali without kindling a light to welcome Lakshmi, the goddess of prosperity. In India, village potters prepare thousands of small bowls for use as lamps. Indian potters get clay from a nearby riverbed, lake, pond, or tank. But you can get your clay from an art supply center or a toy store.

Follow the instructions below to make a clay lantern for Diwali.

Materials

- enough clay for a ball about the size of your hand

- a candle, approximately 4 inches high

- decorations such as bits of colored gravel, like the kind used in a fish tank; small seashells; beach glass; buttons; colored yarn; pasta stars; or any other decorative odds and ends

Make a Lantern for Diwali

Instructions

1. Use a rolling pin or the palm of your hand to flatten the clay into a circle about 5 inches in diameter.

2. Fold up the edges and pinch the sides to form a bowl.

3. Gently press decorations around the outside of the bowl. If you are using yarn, wind it around the outside of the bowl and finish by pressing the ends into the clay. Or, using a pointed object such as a pencil, poke a series of small holes around the sides.

4. Press a candle into the center of the bowl, making sure it sticks firmly.

5. Finally, set your Diwali lamp on a table near the window. At night-fall, have an adult light the candle for you.
   Make sure the lamp is not near any curtains or other flammable material.

India's natural resources made it very attractive to more powerful countries. Both France and Great Britain wanted India's wealth for themselves. The Europeans explored India and began to set up trading posts there. Great Britain opened its first trading post in 1611. The East India Company, which controlled the sale of trade goods such as tea and textiles, soon became powerful enough to set up its own army. In 1857, Indian soldiers working for the company rebelled against their British officers. The mutiny convinced Great Britain to seize power over all of India and its wealth. The country became a British colony and remained under British rule until after World War II. On August 15, 1947, Indians, led by Mahatma Gandhi, won self-rule from Britain.

Republic Day
January 26

On January 26, 1950, India adopted a new constitution. It became a sovereign, democratic republic completely free of British rule. Today all Indians celebrate Republic Day, January 26, with feasts and fairs. In New Delhi, the nation's capital, there is a special parade presided over by the president of India.

A parade celebrating India's independence

Mahatma Gandhi, Peaceful Protester

In 1925, Mohandas K. Gandhi became the leader of the Indian National Congress. This group was formed to gain self-rule for India. Gandhi, a lawyer trained in London, England, believed in achieving this goal through non-violent resistance to British rule. Gandhi asked Indians to boycott, or refuse to buy, British-made goods. Instead, he encouraged people to wear Indian-made clothing and buy Indian-made goods. He also organized peaceful protests. One time, Gandhi walked hundreds of miles to protest a British tax on essential items such as salt. At other times, he fasted to call the world's attention to the plight of Indians. Since Gandhi's followers were unarmed and peaceful, the British were reluctant to attack them and usually only sent them to prison. Out of respect for his simple lifestyle and nonviolent philosophy, the people gave Gandhi the title *Mahatma*, which means "Great Soul." Sadly, Gandhi was assassinated in 1948, only a year after India gained its independence and two years before it became a republic.

Holi, the Spring Festival

A favorite festival of Indians young and old is filled with fun and laughter. Holi celebrates the return of spring with tricks and jokes. It is held in February or March on a night when the moon is full and bright. According to legend, the lord Krishna and his friend Radha first played holi by splashing each other with water. It is customary at Holi for people to throw colored powders and splash colored water on each other. Everyone gets splashed with bright colors such as pink, green, red, orange, and blue. Holi pranks include lowering hooks from windows to snatch the scarves off unsuspecting strollers as they pass on the street below. Another favorite Holi prank is to leave an empty wallet on the street for others to find. It is traditional for the first one who picks up the wallet to give the prankster a bit of money.

Brightly colored powders for Holi

*A bonfire at
a Holi festival*

One popular legend of Holi tells the story of Prahlada, a young boy who worshiped the gods faithfully in spite of the opposition of his father, King Hiranyakasipu. The king desired to be worshiped as a god himself, but the boy would not be put off from his devotion, even in the face of his father's demands and threats. Finally, King Hiranyakasipu called upon the demoness Holika to help him kill the boy. The demoness could walk unharmed through fire, so Hiranyakasipu built a bonfire and asked her to carry Prahlada into it. But the gods heard the wicked king's plan. Because of her evil intentions, Holika was burned to ashes in the fire, but loyal Prahlada lived.

At Holi the destruction of evil is celebrated by the lighting of bonfires in which straw figures in the form of the demoness Holika are burned. Friends and family visit each other, eat, drink, and dance joyfully.

In the past, most Indian families were very large. The children helped their mother and father farm the land and cared for their parents in old age. Today, this traditional lifestyle continues in much of rural India. Raksha Bandhan celebrates the bond between sister and brother. *Raksha bandhan* means "tying for protection" in Hindi. The celebration is held during July or August. Sisters tie colorful ornamental bracelets called *rakhi* on the

Raksha Bandhan: Ties of Protection

wrists of their brothers. The rakhi are considered lucky charms that will protect the wearers from harm. Brothers wear the rakhi as a sign of their pledge to protect their sisters.

On the day of Raksha Bandhan, a ceremonial tying may be performed. A brother sits cross-legged before his sister on a small wooden stool or plank. His sister then marks his forehead with turmeric, a yellow-colored spice, or red powder. She ties the rakhi on his right wrist and feeds him a sweet. The brother may then give his sister a gift of money.

If brother and sister cannot be together on Raksha Bandhan, the rakhi can be tied by a stand-in. If a girl has no brother, she can adopt one by tying a rakhi on a male cousin or friend. But the tying of a rakhi means a serious obligation. An ancient Indian legend tells the story of the princess who, as a child, sent a rakhi to the Mogul emperor. Years later, when her kingdom was invaded, the princess called upon the emperor for help. He sent his troops to assist her without a moment's thought.

Today, rakhi can be made out of anything, from sewing thread to silver and jewels! One common type of rakhi is a bracelet of woven gold and silver threads with a small cotton pom-pom or other decoration in the center. Try making a rakhi, or friendship bracelet, from embroidery thread and some spare buttons you may have at home. Or perhaps you will want to tie-dye a rakhi, using the instructions on pages 34–35.

GAMES

Kabaddi is one of the national pastimes of India. It is played throughout the country. In some places, it is called a different name. Whatever Indians call it, Kabaddi is a tag game with a twist. Taggers must hold their breath while trying to tap their opponents. With players tackling each other to the ground, Kabaddi can get pretty rough at times! Perhaps that's why it is usually played by teenage boys. Since Kabaddi requires only a field to run on, a minimum of six players, and an umpire, the game can be played almost anywhere, at any time. In some villages, more formal Kabaddi tournaments are held. Players compete for trophies and prizes.

Kabaddi

Kabaddi requires two teams: the raiders and the defenders. A line is drawn down the middle of the playing area to separate the territories of each team. The raiders try to reduce the size of the defenders' team by tagging players out. The catch is that raiders may only tag out defending players while they are holding their breath. While they are in enemy territory, raiders must repeat the nonsense word *kabaddi* over and over again, until they run out of breath. A raider who is caught breathless in the defenders' territory is eliminated from play. Then the two teams switch roles for the next round. Games may be timed. Or each side may be given an equal number of raids per team until all the players of one team are eliminated.

Players compete in a national Kabaddi tournament.

Ghora Baddi, an easier version of Kabaddi, is popular with younger players. There are two teams, raiders and defenders. The object of the game is for the raiders to free one of their members from a "jail" behind the home line of the opposing team by tagging out defenders.

To Play You Will Need

- **A playing field.** At each end of the field a "home" line should be marked off with chalk, flour, or paint. Behind each home line, a box should be drawn for captured players to stand or sit in. This is the "jail."

- **Two teams, Raiders and Defenders, with an equal number of players on each side.** The suggested minimum is three on each side, but the game will be more exciting if there are a greater number of players.

Ghora Baddi

How the Raiders Play

(1) The raiders select a member of their team to be the captive in the jail circle on the defenders' side.

(2) The raiders choose the order in which they will send runners into the defenders' territory. Only one raider may be active at a time.

(3) The raider whose turn it is takes a deep breath, runs into the defenders' territory, and attempts to tag a defender out while shouting *baddi, baddi, baddi.* The raider is out if he or she has to take another breath before reaching home again.

(4) When the defenders' team has been reduced in size by tag-outs, it is time for the captive to try to escape from jail without being tagged. The active raider from the captive's team tries to help by chasing the defenders that pursue the captive.

How the Defenders Play

1. Defenders must simultaneously guard the captive while staying clear of the active raider by running and dodging. Once tagged, they cannot get back in the game unless revived (see Other Rules).

2. When a raider tags a defender, the defender's teammates pursue the raider. They can tag the raider only if he or she runs out of *baddi's* (and has to take another breath) before escaping back across the dividing line.

3. Defenders also chase the escaping captive. If the captive is tagged, he or she must return to jail. If a defender is tagged by the active raider, he or she is out.

Other Rules

1. A raider or a defender eliminated by a member of the opposing team may be returned to play in a succeeding inning. Teammates should be revived in the order in which they were out.

2. An inning is over when a captive tries to escape. The teams switch sides and another round begins. If the captive succeeds in escaping back home without being tagged, the raiders score a point. But if the captive is tagged, the defenders score a point.

3. Raiders and defenders should decide in advance how many innings they wish to play. The games cannot end until each side has had an equal number of innings as raiders. The team with the most points wins.

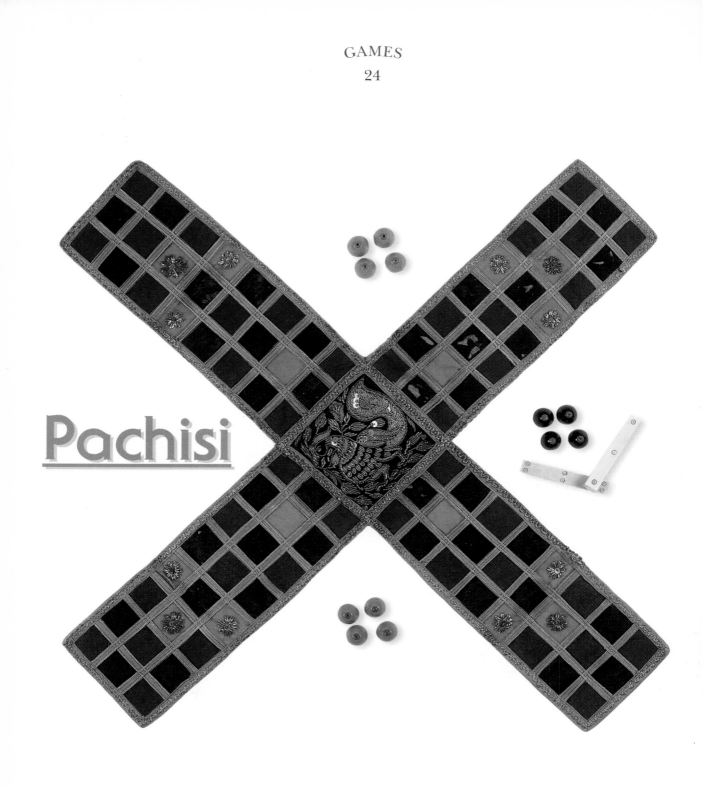

Pachisi

The board game Pachisi (known as Parcheesi in the United States) has been played in India since the sixteenth century and possibly even earlier. Pachisi's popularity has continued throughout the history of India, right into the present day. The Mogul emperor Akbar, who ruled India in the 1500s, had a giant game board in the courtyard of his palace. Servants dressed in the game's colors of red, yellow, green, and black walked around the board as real-life playing pieces.

Versions of Pachisi are played throughout the world.

Pawa Duree is a simple version of Pachisi. It is a game for two to four players that can be played on paper or with chalk on pavement. The object of the game is to be the first player to get four playing pieces to the center of the "board." The number of spaces a piece may be moved is determined by the throw of the four half-bean "dice" that are easy to make.

Follow the instructions below to make your own Pawa Duree game. Be sure to have enough playing pieces for up to four players.

Pawa Duree

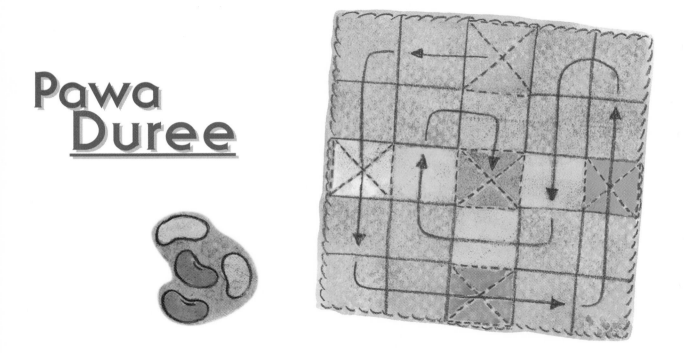

Materials

- pencil and paper to copy the playing board shown here

- a set of four playing pieces per person—colored buttons (4 red, 4 yellow, 4 green, 4 black) or homemade colored paper circles may be used

- two black or red beans that have each been split lengthwise into two parts (half-bean "dice") so that one side is white and the other side is colored

To Set Up

1. Determine who will go first by tossing the bean dice. Scoring is as follows.

   One white and three colored = 1 point
   Two white and two colored = 2 points
   Three white and one colored = 3 points
   Four white = 4 points plus an extra turn
   Four colored = 8 points plus an extra turn

2. Each player chooses a color and places his or her four playing pieces on one of the four outside Xs of the playing board. If only two people are playing, they should start at opposite sides of the board. Each player starts his or her pieces from the same opening square.

To Play

1. The first player throws the bean dice and, following the arrow trail, moves a playing piece the number of spaces indicated.

2. As the game continues, players may move any one of their playing pieces. It is not necessary to move one piece all the way to the center of the board before starting another.
   Note: Only one playing piece may be moved per turn.

3. By landing on a square already occupied by an opponent's playing piece, a player may send that piece back to the beginning. The active player then gets another turn. However, if the active player lands on one of the five Xs, the opponent remains safe and the two playing pieces "share" the space. The active player does not get another turn.

4. If a player throws four or eight points, he or she gets an extra turn (but only for the same playing piece).

5. An exact number of moves is not required to reach the center.

6. The first person to get all four playing pieces to the center wins the game.

This game is a combination of jacks and pick-up sticks. In areas along India's coast, it is played with brightly colored shells called cowrie shells. In other regions, it is played with small stones. For cowrie shells, you can substitute pasta shells. Pebbles or other small objects (like Lego pieces) can also be used to play, as long as five of them will fit into the palm of your hand.

Any number of players may join in playing Five Shells.

To Play

1. Players sit cross-legged on the ground in a circle. Determine which player will go first.

2. The first player spills or tosses the five "shells" in a pile.

3. The player must pick up a shell from the pile without making any of the other shells move. If the player succeeds, he or she then tosses the playing piece up in the air and with the same hand, scoops up a playing piece from the remaining pile before catching the one that was tossed.

Five
Shells

4. If the player has been successful in removing all the shells from the pile, on the next toss he or she must pick up two shells, being careful to move only the pieces being retrieved. If successful, the player tosses the two shells up in the air and scoops up two pieces, and then the remaining piece with the same hand.

5. Any time a player moves a shell or misses a scoop, his or her turn is ended and the next player takes a turn. When all players have had a turn, the first player goes again, beginning with the number of shells he or she missed on the last turn. The winner is the first one to pick up all five shells and catch them in the air.

Each culture has ways of decorating the body. Some people paint their lips; others polish their nails in bright colors. The Indian way of self-decoration is unique. Indian women place a bright red dot called a *tika* on their forehead. The tika is used as a mark of faith. It is also considered a sign of respect for the intellect and is worn by married women as a symbol of devotion

Mehndi: Hand Painting

to their husbands. Others place an ornament in their nose or they wear a colorful sari. These decorations and clothes are readily recognizable as Indian. The intricate Indian art of mehndi hand painting is not so different from some Western customs such as nail polishing or tattooing.

Mehndi hand decoration is most common in northern India. It symbolizes love and friendship. *Mehndi* is the Hindu word for the henna plant from which the dye is obtained. Mehndi designs are worn on special holidays and occasions. They are especially popular for weddings. The designs are most easily applied by placing stencils on the palm of the hand. The henna dye is then spread over the stencil. When the stencil is removed, a design appears on the hand. Sometimes, artists skilled in freehand painting are hired to paint their own designs. These artists squeeze the henna paste through plastic tubes in much the same way that pastry chefs decorate cakes.

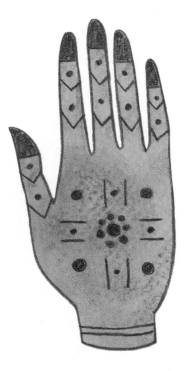

Look at the suggestions shown here for freestyle designs to paint on the hands of classmates and friends. You can purchase henna powder in Indian groceries and specialty shops. If it is not available, try nontoxic, washable paints or markers.

Imagine making a beautiful design for your family and friends, only to have it blown away in the breeze or stepped upon by busy passersby. It's all part of the art of floor painting, which is still practiced today by women all over India. Although floor painting is known by many different names — *kolam* in the south of India, *rangoli* in Maharashtra, *chita* in Orissa, *alpona* in Bengal, *aripana* in Bihar, *sona rakhna* in Uttar Pradesh, *sathiya* in Gujarat, *aripona* in other regions of northern India, and *apna* in the western Himalayas—floor painting is a living tradition that has been handed down from mother to daughter since ancient times.

Rangoli: Floor Painting

A floor painting is usually created at the threshold, or front door, of a home. The painting itself may be a simple geometric design. Or it may tell a story with drawings of flowers, birds, the sun and moon, animals, gods, goddesses, and people. The purpose of floor painting is sometimes decorative and sometimes religious. During festivals, such as Onam in Kerala or Diwali in the north, the paintings may be particularly intricate.

In the south of India, floor paintings are created twice daily, at dawn and dusk throughout the year. But through most of India, floor painting is done as part of a holiday celebration.

The materials used in floor painting vary. In some places sand is used to make a design, and in others the main ingredient is rice powder. These substances may be dyed brilliant colors or left in their natural shades of white or tan.

To make the floor painting, the sand or powder is sifted between the thumb and fingers, a skill that takes many years to learn. In Madbuhani, Bihar, where floor painting is done with rice paste, a kind of finger-painting technique is used. Today, stencil cones for "rolling out" floor paintings are available in markets to save busy Indian women time.

Make a Floor Painting

If you've decided to celebrate Diwali this year, you may want to make a floor painting in honor of Lakshmi, the goddess of good fortune. Or perhaps you'll want to begin a new tradition and create a floor painting to celebrate the birthday of a classmate, teacher, or friend.

Floor painting is fun, but it can be messy. Be sure to have the permission of a teacher or parent before you begin. (Do not try floor painting on a carpet!)

Materials

- a small bag of sand or rice flour
- a well-swept doorstep, or a linoleum, tile, or wooden floor
- paper and pencil
- chalk

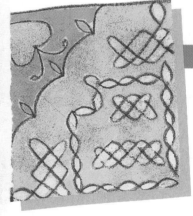

Directions

1. Plan your design using paper and pencil. It is a good idea not to start with anything too complicated. You may want to use the design ideas shown here.

2. Once you have decided upon a design, chalk it lightly on the doorstep or floor.

3. Following your chalk lines, sift the sand or rice flour through your thumb and fingers in a thin steady stream. This will take practice and patience!

4. Remember to clean up after you've shown off and enjoyed your work.

Tie-dyeing is an important part of the cultural heritage of India. For generations, entire communities in western and central India, especially in Gujarat and Rajasthan, have practiced this craft. Each colony of artisans has its own techniques to produce beautiful, specialized designs. Yet basic tie-dyeing is a simple craft that Indian children learn to do in school and at home. Create your own tie-dyed fabric to use when making one of the rakhi described on page 19.

Tie-Dyeing

Materials

- a white 100 percent cotton handkerchief, at least 12 inches square
- three packages of dye in red, yellow, and blue
- four large plastic basins to mix dye and rinse
- marbles, dried chickpeas, or lentils
- box of plastic sandwich bags
- rubber bands

Instructions

1. Mix dye according to package directions.

2. For a simple striped design, accordion-pleat the handkerchief (like a paper fan).

3. Select four rubber bands. Starting at one end of the pleated handkerchief, tightly wind a rubber band around it. Wind the next rubber band three inches below the first. Follow these directions with the remaining two bands.

4. Dip the handkerchief in colored dye. Let it soak for several minutes. The longer it soaks, the darker the color will be.

5. Rinse the colored handkerchief in cold water and allow it to dry.

6. To make a circle pattern, put the marbles, chickpeas, or lentils in the center of the cloth. Wrap and wind tightly with a rubber band. Add several more bands below the first.

7. Dip in dye and then rinse as indicated on package.

8. When dry, new knots may be added. Dip the handkerchief in a second color. Repeat the procedure for a third color. Then let dry completely.

Use your tie-dyed handkerchief to make a *rakhi*. Cut the fabric into half-inch strips. Twist a strip tightly and tie the ends with gold or silver thread. To keep it from unrolling, tie in two or three more places along the length of the bracelet. Your rakhi is ready to tie on!

The *Ramayana (The Story of Rama)* is one of the great epic tales of India. It was written around 200 B.C. It tells the story of the godlike Prince Rama, whose adventures represent the triumph of good over evil. The children of India enjoy reading this exciting tale.

The Exile of Rama

King Dasrath was getting old. He wanted to see his eldest son Rama, whose mother was Kaushalya, named as his successor. But King Dasrath had four wives. One of them, Queen Kaikeyi, fearing that her own son Bharat would be mistreated by Rama, reminded King Dasrath of the two wishes he had once pledged to grant her. Now she demanded that Rama be banished into the forest for 14 years and that Bharat be made successor to the throne instead.

A carved wooden statue of Rama

King Dasrath was heartbroken, but he would never go back on a promise. He was forced to grant Kaikeyi's wishes. The king called Rama to him, but when the young man arrived, his father was too distraught to even speak. Kaikeyi delivered the news instead.

"Long ago, your father granted me two wishes and now he has agreed to fulfill them. You will live in exile in the forest for 14 years. In your place, Bharat will be named successor to the throne."

Rama did not become angry or upset. He understood it was his sacred duty to respect his father's wishes. As calmly and respectfully as ever, he bowed to Kaikeyi. "I will gladly go."

When Rama told his wife, Sita, the news, she said, "I will also go with you." In order to dissuade her, Rama described the dangers and hardships of life in the forest. But Sita insisted. "The duty of a wife is to be by the side of her husband. I will never be at peace without you."

At last, Rama agreed to let Sita accompany him. As he prepared to leave, the news of his exile reached his brother Lakshman. The loyal brother insisted upon accompanying Rama as well. "It is my duty as a brother to honor and protect you," Lakshman said. Rama saw that he could not change his brother's mind, so together the three exiles set out for the forest.

Rama, Sita, and Lakshman leave for their exile in the forest.

Ravan Seeks Revenge

While Rama, Sita, and Lakshman were living in the forest, they had to fight many demons. During one of these battles, Rama killed the demoness Surpnakha, sister of the ten-headed demon king, Ravan. Ravan was very angry. To punish Rama, he decided to kidnap Sita and marry her himself.

Rama chasing the golden deer

Ravan sent his magician, Mareech, into the forest to search for Sita. When the magician finally found her, he turned himself into a golden deer. Sita was so entranced by the beautiful animal that she said to Rama, "I must have that wondrous creature!"

But Lakshman warned, "It must be a trick. There is no such animal as a golden deer. I beg you, do not go after it."

Rama ignored his advice. He wanted to capture the animal for his dear wife. Before he set off to catch it, he commanded Lakshman to guard Sita. "Never leave her alone," he warned. Then he disappeared into the forest.

Soon after Rama was gone, the evil Ravan began calling for help in the voice of Rama. Sita heard his cries and shouted to Lakshman, "Brother, run! You must save Rama!"

"Perhaps it is a trick—the voice of a demon," Lakshman replied. "I have promised Rama not to leave you alone."

Sita became very angry. "If something happens to Rama, I will die, too. You must go and help him at once!"

Lakshman was torn between Rama's orders and his fear for his brother's safety. Finally, he drew a circle around the entrance of the hut. "Do not step beyond this charmed circle and no harm will come to you," he told Sita. Still feeling reluctant to leave her, he set off to search for his brother.

All the while, Ravan had been hiding behind a tree and watching. He had to think of a way to make Sita step out of the charmed circle. He dressed as a holy man and approached the hut, carrying a begging bowl.

In the house of Rama, holy men were always welcome. As soon as Sita saw the man, she brought out some food to offer him. As she did so, she stepped beyond the charmed circle. Immediately, Ravan grabbed her and carried her away to Lanka (Sri Lanka today) in his magic chariot.

When Rama and Lakshman found out what had happened to Sita, they began a great journey to rescue her. After many adventures, they reached the kingdom of Lanka, where they fought three great battles to win Sita's freedom.

◊　◊　◊　◊

The *Ramayana* contains many thrilling stories of the exploits of Rama and Lakshman as they sought to rescue Sita. Your local library may have a children's retelling of the *Ramayana* in which you can read more.

The *Mahabharata* is said to be the longest epic tale in the world. It was written between 200 B.C. and A.D. 200 and is made up of 18 books. Through a series of episodes, it relates the struggle between two royal families, the Pandavs and the Kauravs, to rule the kingdom of Hastinapur. But the *Mahabharata* is more than a collection of thrilling adventures. For centuries, Indian parents and teachers have used its stories to help teach their children values. "Bheem and Baku" is one of those stories.

B h e e m   a n d   B a k u

The five Pandav brothers—Yudhishtra the wise, Bheem the strong, Arjun the great warrior, and the twins Nakul and Sahadeve—discovered that their cousin Duryodhan was plotting to have them killed. Together with their mother, Kunti, they escaped to the forest and wandered until they came to the city of Ekchakra. A kind man recognized them and invited them to stay at his house. The desperate Pandavs thankfully accepted the invitation.

A Tale From the Mahabharata

Every day, the brothers dressed as poor but holy men and went out to beg for food. In the evening, they brought what they had collected to Kunti, who divided the food into five portions. Bheem was given the largest share because he was very big and strong and always hungry.

One morning, Kunti overheard their kind host speaking to his wife and little boy. The woman and child began to weep. Kunti went in and asked, "Please tell me what is wrong. Perhaps my sons can help you."

The kind man shook his head. "About ten years ago, a rakshasa (an ogre) named Baku came to live in a cave near our city. For food, he caught many people at a time and ate them. The citizens of Ekchakra became desperate. Finally, they went to the rakshasa to make a deal.

"'If you keep eating us, there will soon be no more for you to eat,' they said. 'Why not stay in your cave and let us send a cart full of food to you each week. The cart will be drawn by two bullocks, and each household will take turns sending a driver. You can eat the

food, the bullocks, and the driver, too.'

"The rakshasa agreed. Since then, a man is eaten each week. Now it is my turn," the man said sadly.

"But why haven't the people killed Baku?" Kunti asked.

"Many brave men have tried," the man explained, "but he has eaten them all."

"Do not go to his cave," Kunti told the man. "I will send one of my sons instead. God will help him."

Kunti went to her sons and told them about the rakshasa. "I can kill him!" Bheem declared. "Tell our host I will take his place."

The next morning Bheem set out with the cart full of food and the bullocks. But he was always hungry. He ate all the food on his way to the cave, but he kept on going. When he got there, he called, "Baku, come get your lunch!"

The rakshasa came out of his cave and looked at the empty cart. "Where is my food?" he roared.

"I've eaten it."

Baku leered at Bheem. "No matter. You're big and fat and will fill me up all the same."

"Not unless you can kill me," Bheem told him.

"What? I always eat the driver!" thundered Baku.

"First you must fight me," Bheem insisted.

Baku laughed. He tore a tree out of the ground and threw it, but Bheem just brushed it away. He pounded Bheem with his fists, but Bheem just laughed. Then Bheem picked up the rakshasa and threw him down on the ground. He stamped on Baku until his bones were all broken and he was dead.

Bheem carried Baku's body to the city where the people rejoiced. Then he went home and washed himself. His mother was proud of his great deed.

In this painting the mighty Bheem is attacking the Kauravs.

The foods of India are as varied as its languages, religions, customs, and dress. Indian cooking is based on foods that are grown in each region. Ethnic ties, religious customs, and lifestyles also determine what Indians eat. But there is one thing all Indians have in common: spice! Indian cooks are the spice artists of the world.

Many newcomers to Indian cooking wrongly think that Indian food is hot and requires big gulps of water between bites. Actually, most of the spices used by Indian cooks are not hot at all, just extremely flavorful. Although chilies, or hot peppers, are used

in some dishes, a cook can always add more or less to please the taste of his or her guests. The recipes that follow are a mild introduction to the tastes of India. Enjoy.

Chapati is a flat, individual-sized bread eaten in most of northern India. It may be served warm with a little butter or as an accompaniment to dishes such as aloo mattar. The chapati is prepared in a way that is similar to making a Mexican tortilla, except for the last step when it is puffed up like an edible cloud.

Ingredients

- 2½ cups chapati flour (available in Indian and Pakistani markets) or 1¾ cups sifted whole wheat flour plus ¾ cup unbleached white flour
- extra flour for dusting hands, work surface, and rolling pin
- ¾ cup water

Utensils

- measuring cups
- bowl
- mixing spoon
- board or other surface for kneading dough
- dishcloth
- rolling pin
- tava (a slightly concave, castiron pan) or heavy frying pan
- tongs

Directions

Always have an adult with you when using the stove or range top!

1. Put the flour in a bowl and slowly add the water. Mix together to form a soft dough.

2. Knead the dough for about eight minutes. When it is smooth, put the dough back in the bowl and cover it with a clean damp dishcloth. Let it sit for $\frac{1}{2}$ hour.

3. Begin heating the tava or frying pan. Meanwhile, knead the dough once more.

4. Dust hands, board, and rolling pin with flour. Pinch off enough dough to roll into a "meatball" and place on work surface. Flatten into a circle with the palm of your hand.

5. Roll out the dough ball into a circle about 5 inches in diameter. Slap the chapati onto the hot frying pan. (Do not use oil!)

6. After about $1\frac{1}{2}$ minutes, turn the chapati over with the tongs. Cook for another $\frac{1}{2}$ minute.

7. Remove the frying pan from the range top. Turn the flame down to low, and with the tongs place the chapati directly on the burner over the flame. After a few seconds, the chapati will puff up. Now turn the chapati over and let it sit for 2 to 3 more seconds. Remove it from the heat, add butter, and eat immediately.

This potato dish is very tasty and slightly hot. It goes well with chicken or beef but is often served as part of a vegetarian meal. Aloo mattar also makes an excellent lunch, especially when eaten with chapati.

To Set Up

- 2 tablespoons peanut oil
- 1 green chili pepper, chopped
- 1 teaspoon chopped fresh ginger
- 1 clove garlic, chopped
- 1 small onion, chopped
- $\frac{1}{2}$ teaspoon salt
- 3 medium potatoes, peeled and chopped
- 2 cups water
- 10-ounce package frozen peas (optional)
- $\frac{1}{2}$ cup toasted cashew nuts, chopped

Utensils

- 10-inch frying pan with cover
- spatula
- mixing spoon
- measuring cups
- serving bowl

Directions

**Always have an adult with
you when using the stove or range top!**

1. Pour the peanut oil into the pan and heat. Add the chili, ginger, garlic, onion, and salt and cook over medium heat for 3 to 4 minutes until the mixture turns a golden color.

2. Stir in the potatoes. Add water and bring to a boil. Cover the pan and lower the heat. The mixture should simmer about 20 minutes until the potatoes are tender and the water is mostly absorbed. If including peas, add these during the last three minutes of cooking.

3. Remove the mixture from the heat and scrape it into a serving bowl. Sprinkle toasted cashews on top and serve.

Indians use a variety of fresh vegetables in their cooking.

Burfee is a fudgelike candy that is rich and delicious. Although this recipe is for coconut burfee, Indian cooks make many different kinds, such as cashew, pistachio, carrot, and even chocolate. Once you know the basic recipe, you can create your own variations, too. You can find cardamom in the spice section of the local supermarket.

Ingredients

- 2 teaspoons butter
- $\frac{1}{2}$ pound ricotta cheese
- $1\frac{1}{2}$ cups powdered milk
- 1 cup shredded coconut
- $1\frac{1}{2}$ cups sugar
- 6 green cardamom pods, crushed, or $\frac{1}{2}$ teaspoon ground cardamom
- 1 teaspoon rose water (optional but adds a wonderfully exotic scent)

Coconut Burfee

Some tempting Indian sweets

Utensils

- measuring cups and spoons
- bowl
- mixing spoon
- 8-inch to 10-inch frying pan
- glass or metal baking pan, greased

Directions

Always have an adult with you when using the stove or range top!

1. Melt the butter in a large frying pan. Add the ricotta cheese and stir continuously over low heat for ten minutes. The cheese will begin to develop a dry consistency.

2. While stirring continuously, slowly sprinkle in the powdered milk. If the mixture seems too dry, add a tablespoon of water or fresh milk. Stir for five minutes.

3. Mix in the coconut. Stir for another five minutes and add sugar. Cook until the mixture is quite dry (about five minutes).

4. Remove the mixture from the heat and stir in the cardamom and rose water. Pour the mixture into a greased pan and press down flat. Allow it to cool and then refrigerate.

5. After two hours, remove the burfee from the refrigerator and cut into squares or diamond shapes. Serve and enjoy.

Bibliography

The Asia Societfy. *India, a Teacher's Guide.* New York: The Asia Society, 1985.

Bernard, Nicholas. *Arts and Crafts of India.* London: Conran Octopus Limited, 1993.

Choudhry, Bani Roy. *The Story of Ramayan, the Epic Tale of India.* New Delhi: Hemkunt Press, 1970.

Games of the World. Geneva: Swiss Committee for UNICEF, 1975.

Smithsonian Institution. *Aditi: The Living Arts of India.* Washington, D.C.: Smithsonian Institution Press, 1986.

Tagore, Rabindranath. *The Collected Poems and Plays of Rabindranath Tagore.* New York: The Macmillan Company, 1962.

About the Author

Phyllis Shalant lives in Westchester, New York. Her other books for Julian Messner include *Look What We've Brought You From Korea, Look What We've Brought You From Mexico,* and *Look What We've Brought You From Vietnam.*

INDEX

Akbar, king, 9, 25
aloo mattar, 44-45
arts, 30-35
Aryans, 9
Asoka, king, 9

Bombay, 7
Buddhism, 9
burfee, 46-47

Calcutta, 7
chapati, 42-43
Christianity, 9

Diwali (Festival of Lights), 11-13, 32, 33

families, 6, 18
five shells, 28
floor painting, 32-33
foods, 7, 42-47
France, 14

games, 6, 20-28
Gandhi, Mohandas K., 9, 14, 15
Ganges River, 7
Ghora Baddi, 6, 22-23
gods and goddesses, 10, 11, 12, 17
Great Britain, 9, 14-15

henna, 30
Hinduism, 6, 9, 10-11
Holi, 16-17
holidays and festivals, 6, 10-13, 14, 16-17, 18-19

India
    capital city, 7
    cities, 7
    climate, 7
    flag, 9
    history, 7-9, 14-15
    languages, 6, 7
    location, 7
    map, 8
    population, 6, 7
    religions, 6, 9
    self-rule and independence, 9, 14-15
    size, 7
    states, 7
Indian Americans, 6
Indian National Congress, 9, 15
Islam, 9

Kabaddi, 20-22
Kumbha Mela, 7

Lakshmi, 11-12, 33
legends and stories, 17, 18-19, 36-41

Mahabharata, 40-41
mehndi (hand painting), 30-31
melas (fairs), 10
Mogul Empire, 9, 25
monsoons, 7, 11

New Delhi, 7, 14

Pachisi, 24-26
Parcheesi. *See* Pachisi.
Pawa Duree, 26-27
projects
    floor painting, 33
    lantern for Diwali, 12-13
    Pawa Duree game, 26-27
    recipes, 42-47
    tie-dyeing, 34-35

rakhi, 18-19, 34-35
Raksha Bandhan, 6, 18-19
Ramayana (The Story of Rama), 36-39
rangoli, 32-33
Republic Day, 14

tie-dying, 34-35
tika, 30

utsavas (religious festivals), 10